Rabl

MW01469218

Written by Ed Stanley

Celebration Press
Parsippany, New Jersey

Rabbits eat lettuce . . .

and spinach . . .

and radishes . . .

and carrots . . .

and peas . . .

and even flowers!

Yum!

Thinking Back

1. What kinds of things do rabbits like to eat?

2. What other foods do you think rabbits would enjoy eating?

3. Where do you think the rabbits find all of these foods?

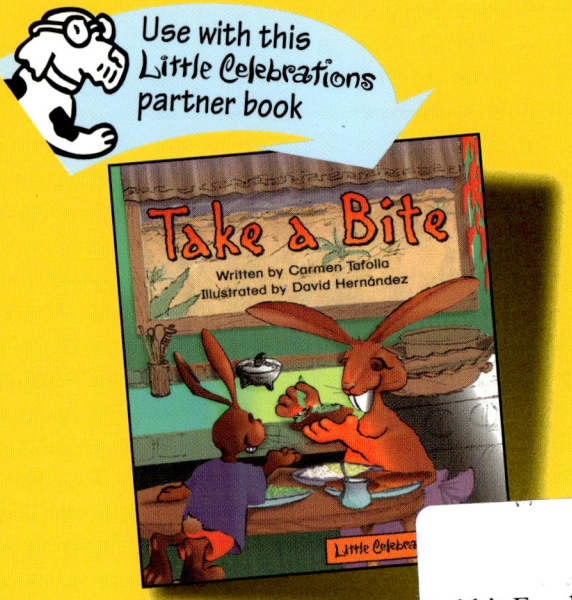

Use with this
Little Celebrations
partner book

Take a Bite

Written by Carmen Tafolla
Illustrated by David Hernández

Little Celebrations

Rabbit Food
Level: C

Celebration
Press

An imprint of Pearson Learning

ISBN 0-673-58042-3

90000>

9 780673 580429